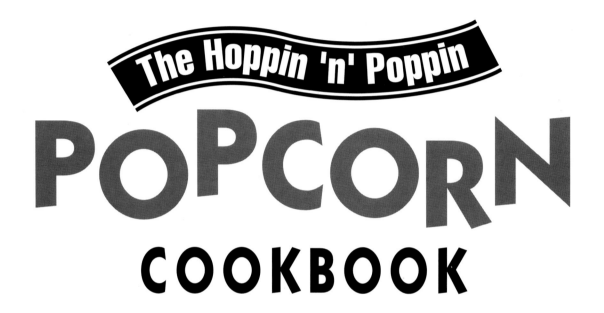

The Hoppin 'n' Poppin
POPCORN
COOKBOOK

The Hoppin 'n' Poppin

POPCORN
COOKBOOK

Gina Steer

THE
APPLE
PRESS

A QUINTET BOOK

Published by The Apple Press
6 Blundell Street
London N7 9BH

ISBN 1-85076-586-3

This book was designed and produced
by Quintet Publishing Limited
6 Blundell Street
London N7 9BH

Creative Director: Richard Dewing
Designer: Mark Roberts @ Design Revolution
Project Editors: Claire Tennant-Scull/Anna Briffa
Photographer: Jeremy Thomas
Food Stylist: Colin Capon

Typeset in Great Britain by
Central Southern Typesetters, Eastbourne
Manufactured in Malaysia by
C.H. Colour Scan Sdn. Bhd.
Printed in Singapore by
Star Standard Industries (Pte) Ltd

Acknowledgements:
The Publisher would like to thank
Swizzels Matlow Ltd for providing
products for photography.

contents

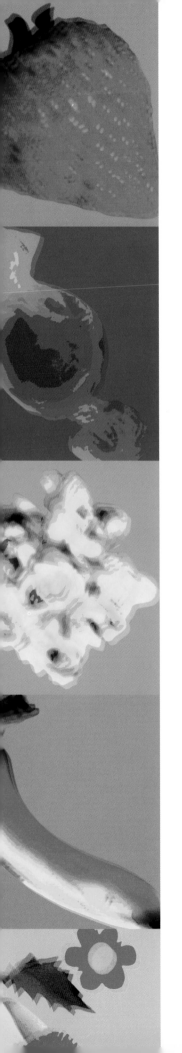

introduction

history

Most people think that popcorn is a modern food, but in fact it has been around for many centuries. The oldest ears of corn were found in Bat Cave, situated in west central Mexico. It was discovered that here the Cochise Indians, dating back to 2,500 B.C., grew and ate popcorn. Scientists now believe that popcorn originated in Mexico. A funeral urn dated about 300 A.D. shows a maize god with some form of primitive popcorn in his head-dress. Preserved grains of popcorn that will still pop were found in tombs on the east coast of Peru and are believed to be 1,000 years old.

the early popcorn

It was the original corn, wild and early cultivated, and the staple diet of the American Indian, that was used both for eating and decoration. At the first Thanksgiving feast in Plymouth, Massachusetts, one of the Chief's brothers arrived with goodwill gifts for the English colonists, of which one was a deerskin bag filled with popped popcorn.

After their introduction to popcorn, the colonists had the idea of eating popcorn with milk and sugar and so breakfast cereal arrived. There were more than 700 varieties of popcorn grown at this time.

Columbus also found the natives in the West Indies eating popcorn as well as using it for decoration. When Cortes invaded Mexico in 1519 he discovered that popcorn was as important to the Aztecs as elsewhere, and was used for decorating their ceremonial head-dresses and necklaces, plus of course it was an integral part of their diet.

early methods of popping

The early consumers of popcorn popped it by toasting it over a fire or even by throwing the cobs into the fire until the corn burst, although many tribes did use clay or metal cooking pots as well. It was the colonists who improved on the Indian cooking vessels and developed a corn popper that was made of thin sheet iron which revolved on an axle in front of the fire. Some of the corn popping vessels that are used in western and central Mexico today are direct descendants of these very early vessels and are used with or without legs or lids and do not necessarily need oil for popping.

Some of the popcorn was still popped on the cob and the kernels remained attached. The Indians would pierce the centre of the cob with a sharp stick then toast on an open fire. These were an immensely popular snack.

It was in the 18th century that popping popcorn in oil really started, as it was discovered that the results and taste were much better than simply toasted.

Popcorn is in fact corn, and although there are five different types of corn grown, popcorn is the only variety that pops. No variety of popcorn is the same and it ranges in colour from off-white to light gold, red, black and a variety of in-between colours.

Once popped, the corn has two basic shapes, snowflake which is large and shaped like a cumulus cloud and mushroom, shaped like a large round ball.

nutritional value of popcorn

Popcorn is a combination of carbohydrate (principally starch), protein, fat and water. The water is stored in the small circle of soft starch.

Popcorn is not just a fun food; like other cereal grains it provides the body with heat and energy. It is now a recognized fact that the body needs about 100 g/4 oz of carbohydrate a day in order to avoid the breakdown in body protein and other undesirable bodily changes. Apart from the carbohydrate content, popcorn is high in fibre and protein and also contains phosphorous and iron. In its natural form, it has no artificial colour, flavouring or additives and is very low in calories. 100 g/4 oz of plain popped popcorn has only 27 grams of calories, if tossed in butter about 126 calories.

Many health and medical groups feel that popcorn provides good nutritional benefits and some weight conscious groups recommend plain popcorn as a valuable substitute for other forms of carbohydrate. It also provides a valuable in-between meal snack if eaten plain as it satisfies the appetite without spoiling it.

why does popcorn pop?

When the kernel is heated, the water inside the kernel heats and the pressure builds up, causing the water to expand and the outer casing to burst. The kernel is then turned inside out and the soft starch pops out as the steam inside is released.

It is down to personal choice whether you pop popcorn in a commercial electric popper, on the stove, in the oven, open fire or even the microwave.

If using a microwave, it is recommended that you use the popcorn that is sold specifically for microwaves; this is because of the packaging. As a microwave concentrates the heat on the largest item, the microwave popcorn is packed as densely as possible to insure maximum popability; this is best done by the packagers themselves, not by the average person popping corn.

If using an electric popper, follow the manufacturer's instructions. Never be tempted to overload the popper because you will not get a good result.

On the stove, for each 25 g/ 1 oz of unpopped popping corn use 30 ml/2 tbsp of oil. First heat the oil in a heavy-based pan of at least 2.25 L/4 pt capacity. Place on a high heat if using electricity or medium for gas. Heat to about 200°C/400°F. You can test the temperature by dropping one or two kernels into the oil. When the kernels spin in the oil it is ready. You need to cover the base of the pan, certainly no more at any

Once the oil has heated, add the corn kernels and immediately cover with a tight-fitting lid. Shake or keep the pan moving constantly (the shaking ensures that each kernel is evenly coated with the oil). The corn will begin to pop within a few seconds. When the kernels have stopped popping, remove from the heat and then wait for at least 1 minute, before removing the lid. Discard any unpopped kernels then coat with your favourite topping or mix.

old maids

If after popping you have any kernels that remain un-popped, discard them. The un-popped kernels are often referred to as Old Maids and do not pop because they are too dry. However, they can be revived by placing them in a jar with water, securing with a tight-fitting lid and leaving for a couple of days, shaking occasionally.

Salt added to popcorn before popping results in tough popcorn, so always add it after popping.

storage

It is important to store popcorn properly. If popcorn is stored in the refrigerator the moisture level can dry out and the popcorn will become soggy.

Store plain popcorn in an airtight container in a cool place or cupboard.

Once popcorn has been mixed with a topping or mix it is advisable to eat it the same day, and if the topping or mix is wet, within 2 to 3 hours.

Popcorn can be coloured and used as decorations, by simply adding food colouring and a little water to the popped popcorn and shaking gently. This will provide fun decorations at parties for both children and adults. For the more adventurous, larger decorations can be fashioned using coloured popcorn which would make a spectacular as well as fun centrepiece for any table.

consumption

Nowadays, most of the popcorn that is consumed is grown in the U.S.A. and although popular throughout the rest of the world, the consumption of popcorn is highest in the States. In 1992, 511,181,000 kg/1,124,600,000 lb of popcorn was consumed; this breaks down to 71 quarts (8 pts) per person.

Most of the popcorn is eaten in the home and of that nearly all is home-popped, mainly with a salt, butter or toffee coating.

But that will become a thing of the past, now that popcorn is recognized as a fun, healthy food. There is a growing demand for many different varieties of toppings and mixes and this book is packed full of tempting ideas that are quick'n'easy to prepare and cook. They provide a host of ideas for every conceivable occasion and unless otherwise stated will serve four or more people as a generous appetizer.

Get popping – popcorn lovers!

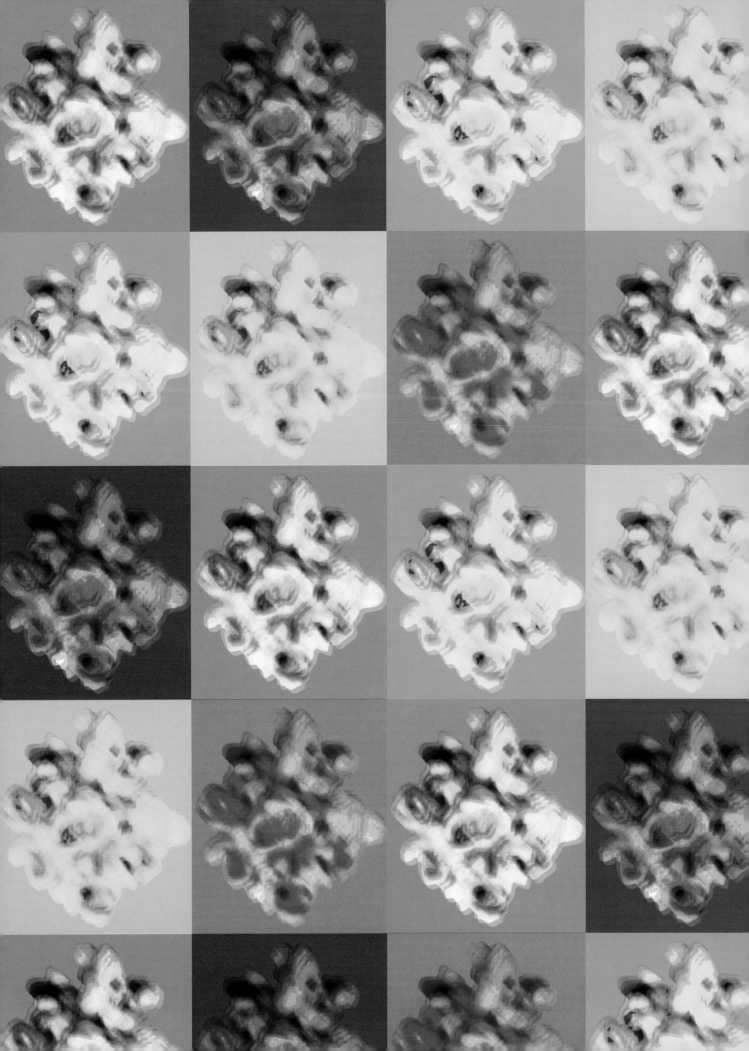

Chapter One

kids' treats

SALTY TEMPTER

THE TRADITIONAL AND POSSIBLY BEST-LOVED WAY OF EATING POPCORN.

MAKES ABOUT 1 LITRE/1¾ PINTS

★ 30 ml/2 tbsp corn or groundnut oil

★ 25 g/1 oz popping corn

Heat the oil in a large heavy-based pan or "popper" and place over a medium heat if using gas, or a high heat if using an electric hob.

Add the popping corn and cover with a tight-fitting lid. Shake gently.

Popping will start within 2 to 3 seconds, so keep the pan moving constantly by shaking it vigorously until the popping has completely stopped.

FOR THE TOPPING

★ 15-20 g/1-1½ tbsp coarsely milled rock salt

Remove the pan from the heat, but do not remove the lid for 1 minute. This will allow any unpopped kernels to pop in the residual heat.

Remove the lid and pour the popcorn into a large bowl and discard any unpopped kernels.

Coarsely grind the salt over the freshly popped popcorn and serve.

BUTTERY GOODIES

THIS HAS TO BE MOST PEOPLE'S ALL-TIME FAVOURITE WAY OF EATING POPCORN.

★ 1 L/1¾ pts freshly popped popcorn

FOR THE TOPPING

★ 3 tbsp/40 g/1½ oz unsalted butter

★ pinch of salt

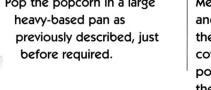

Pop the popcorn in a large heavy-based pan as previously described, just before required.

Melt the butter in a large pan and remove from the heat. Add the freshly popped popcorn and cover. Shake gently until the popcorn is completely coated then sprinkle with salt to taste.

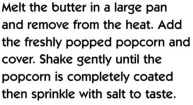

SALT

BUTTER

SuNNy-SIdE SaLAd mIx

**TRY SERVING THIS AS A
SALAD ACCOMPANIMENT AT TEA OR SUPPERTIME.**

★ 1 L/1$^3/_4$ pts freshly popped popcorn
★ pinch of salt

FOR THE MIX
★ 2 ripe tomatoes, peeled, deseeded and finely chopped
★ 5 cm/2 in piece cucumber, peeled and finely chopped

★ 1 carrot, peeled and grated
★ 1 eating apple, cored and finely chopped
★ 15 ml/1 tbsp orange juice
★ 30 g/2 tbsp mint, freshly chopped
★ a few lettuce leaves, to serve

Pop the popcorn in a large heavy-based pan as previously described, just before required. Sprinkle with salt to taste.

Place the tomatoes, cucumber and carrot in a mixing bowl. Toss the apple into the orange juice then add to the tomatoes together with the mint. Mix together lightly.

Stir in the freshly popped popcorn and stir gently.

Arrange the lettuce leaves on individual serving plates then top with the popcorn and tomato mix. Serve immediately.

16

TUNA TREAT

**IF PREFERRED, SERVE WITH
RAW VEGETABLE CRUDITÉS AND TACO CHIPS AS AN
UNUSUAL STARTER OR AT PARTIES.**

★ 1 L/1$^{3}/_{4}$ pts freshly popped popcorn

FOR THE TOPPING

★ 4 spring onions, trimmed and finely chopped

★ 2 celery sticks, trimmed and finely chopped

★ 1 x 99 g/3$^{1}/_{2}$ oz can tuna, drained and finely flaked

★ grated rind of 1 lemon

★ 15 ml/1 tbsp lemon juice

★ 45 ml/3 tbsp mayonnaise

★ spring onion tassels, to garnish

Pop the popcorn in a large heavy-based pan as previously described, just before required.

Mix together the spring onions, celery, tuna and lemon rind and juice. Stir in the mayonnaise. Place the freshly popped popcorn in a large mixing bowl and add the tuna mix.

Stir gently until the popcorn is completely coated and serve immediately. Provide spoons or forks for eating.

17

FiERy tEMPtER

IF FRESNO CHILIES ARE UNAVAILABLE,
YOU CAN USE ANY OTHER FRESH CHILLIES OR EVEN THE JARS
OF FRESHLY MINCED CHILLI AVAILABLE IN THE SUPERMARKET. THE AMOUNT
WILL DEPEND ON YOUR HEAT TOLERANCE, SO START WITH A LITTLE
AND INCREASE ACCORDING TO TASTE.

★ 1 L/$1^3/_4$ pts freshly popped popcorn

FOR THE TOPPING
★ 1 small onion, peeled and sliced
★ 2 cloves of garlic, peeled and sliced

★ 2-3 Fresno red chilli peppers, deseeded and sliced
★ 30 ml/2 tbsp corn or sunflower oil
★ 2 tbsp parsley, freshly chopped
★ salt and freshly ground black pepper

Pop the popcorn in a large heavy-bottomed pan as previously described, just before required.

Place the onion, garlic and chilli in a pestle and mortar or food processor fitted with a metal blade, and either pound or blend to a smooth purée.

Heat the oil in a frying pan and gently sauté the purée for 5 minutes, stirring constantly.

Remove from the heat and stir in the parsley and seasoning to taste. Cool slightly.

Pour over the freshly popped popcorn and stir gently until well coated.

DUTCH SURPRISE

SERVE THIS WITH SALAD AND COLD MEATS AS A FUN, TEA-TIME SALAD.

★ 1 L/1$\frac{3}{4}$ pts freshly popped popcorn

FOR THE TOPPING

★ 25 g/1 oz butter
★ 100 g/4 oz Edam or mature Gouda cheese, finely diced
★ 2.5-5 g/$\frac{1}{2}$-1 tsp dry mustard powder
★ 30 g/2 tbsp chives, freshly snipped

Pop the popcorn in a large heavy-based pan as previously described, just before required.

Melt the butter in a pan then add the cheese and dry mustard powder. Mix together lightly.

Add the freshly popped popcorn to the mix and stir gently with a wooden spoon for 1 to 2 minutes or until the popcorn is completely coated.

Sprinkle on the snipped chives and serve.

19

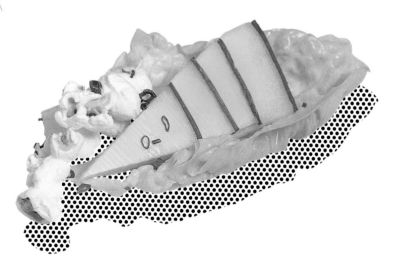

CRUNCHIE SUPPER-TIME

**STUCK FOR AN IDEA FOR SUPPER?
THEN LOOK NO FURTHER. THIS DISH WILL PROVIDE A HEALTHY AND
FILLING SNACK AND BRING A SMILE TO EVERYONE'S LIPS.**

★ 1 l/1$^3/_4$ pts freshly popped popcorn

FOR THE TOPPING

★ 100 g/4 oz streaky bacon, rind removed and coarsely chopped

★ 1 small onion, peeled and finely sliced

★ 50 g/2 oz mushrooms, wiped and finely sliced

Pop the popcorn in a large heavy-based pan as previously described, just before required.

Place the bacon in a non-stick frying pan and place over a gentle heat. Cook gently for 3 to 5 minutes or until the fat begins to run out.

Increase the heat slightly and add the onion. Cook, stirring frequently, for a further 5 minutes or until the onion has softened. Stir in the mushrooms.

Increase the heat and cook for a further 1 to 2 minutes or until the bacon turns crisp.

Remove from the heat and allow to cool before adding to the freshly popped popcorn. Stir gently until completely coated.

20

CHICKEN LICKIN'

FOR A CHANGE SUBSTITUTE TURKEY FOR THE CHICKEN MEAT. EITHER WAY, THIS POPCORN RECIPE IS LOW ON CALORIES, HIGH ON TASTE AND APPEAL.

★ 1 L/1³/₄ pts freshly popped popcorn

FOR THE TOPPING

★ 175 g/6 oz boneless chicken breast

★ 15 ml/1 tbsp sunflower oil
★ 1 tbsp/15 g/¹/₂ oz butter
★ 15 ml/1 tbsp clear honey
★ grated rind of 1 small orange
★ 4 spring onions, trimmed and finely chopped

Pop the popcorn in a large heavy-based pan as previously described, just before required. Place in individual serving bowls.

Discard any skin from the chicken and finely chop or cut into very thin shreds.

Heat the oil and butter in a large frying pan then add the chicken. Sauté for 3 to 5 minutes or until sealed. Add the honey and orange rind and continue to cook for a further 5 minutes or until the chicken is cooked and a light syrup has formed.

Remove from the heat and stir in the spring onions. Spoon the chicken mixture on top of the freshly popped popcorn and serve immediately.

21

MARMITE DELIGHT

THIS SAVOURY TOPPING IS GREAT FOR ALL AGES.

★ 1 L/1³/₄ pts freshly popped popcorn

FOR THE TOPPING
★ 15 ml/1 tbsp corn or sunflower oil
★ 10-15 ml/2-3 tsp marmite

Pop the popcorn in a large heavy-based pan as previously described, just before required.

Place the corn or sunflower oil and marmite in a large pan and heat through, stirring constantly until well blended.

Remove from the heat and allow to cool. Add the freshly popped popcorn to the pan.

Stir gently with a wooden spoon until the popcorn is completely coated in the topping.

22

23

HERBY DELIGHT

VARY THE HERBS ACCORDING TO AVAILABILITY AND PERSONAL PREFERENCE. FRESH HERBS ARE A MUST FOR THIS MIX, DRIED WILL NOT GIVE THE SAME TASTE AND AROMA.

★ 1 L/1$\frac{3}{4}$ pts freshly popped popcorn

FOR THE MIX
★ 45 ml/3 tbsp virgin olive oil
★ 15 g/1 tbsp basil, freshly chopped
★ 15 g/1 tbsp parsley, freshly chopped
★ 15 g/1 tbsp mint, freshly chopped
★ pinch of salt

Pop the popcorn in a large heavy-based pan as previously described, just before required.

Heat the oil in a large pan and add the herbs. Gently sauté for 1 minute stirring frequently.

Remove from the heat and add to the freshly popped popcorn with a pinch of salt to taste. Stir gently with a wooden spoon. Alternatively add the freshly popped popcorn to the pan and cover with a tight-fitting lid and shake gently.

Once the popcorn is completely coated with the herbs, place in a serving bowl and eat either warm or cold.

POPCORN STROGANOFF

IF YOU TRY SERVING THIS AS A VEGETARIAN ALTERNATIVE TO BEEF STROGANOFF, YOU MAY FIND THAT YOUR GUESTS SUDDENLY ALL TURN VEGETARIAN.

★ 1 L/1$\frac{3}{4}$ pts freshly popped popcorn

FOR THE TOPPING
★ 150 ml/$\frac{1}{4}$ pt soured cream
★ 30 g/2 tbsp chives, freshly snipped
★ 1 large orange
★ 50 g/2 oz button mushrooms, wiped and finely chopped
★ 50 g/2 oz mature Cheddar cheese, finely grated
★ salt and freshly ground black pepper

Pop the popcorn in a large heavy-based pan as previously described, just before required.

Place the soured cream in a mixing bowl and mix in the snipped chives.

Grate the orange rind from the orange and divide the orange into segments, discarding the skin. Cut the segments into small pieces then stir the rind and flesh into the soured cream together with the mushrooms. Add the cheese together with the seasoning and stir gently. Place the freshly popped popcorn in a large mixing bowl, add the soured cream topping and mix until the popcorn is completely coated. Serve.

24

MIGHTY MEATIE

IF YOU LOVE BEEFY CHIPS, YOU'LL LOVE THIS POPCORN. YOU JUST WON'T BE ABLE TO EAT ENOUGH.

★ 1 L/1^3/$_4$ pts freshly popped popcorn

FOR THE MIX
★ 30 ml/2 tbsp sunflower or corn oil
★ 15 ml/1 tbsp meat extract (such as Bovril)
★ 2.5 g/^{1}/$_2$ tsp dry mustard powder

Pop the popcorn in a large heavy-based pan as previously described, just before required.

Blend together the oil, meat extract and mustard powder and place in a large pan.

Place over a gentle heat and cook for 1 to 2 minutes stirring once or twice or until blended. Remove from the heat. Add the freshly popped popcorn, cover with a tight-fitting lid and shake the pan vigorously for 1 minute or until the popcorn is completely coated. Eat either warm or cold.

FISHY FUN

TRY SERVING THIS FUN TOPPING ON BAKED POTATOES OR IN TACO SHELLS FILLED WITH SHREDDED LETTUCE.

★ 1 L/1^3/$_4$ pts freshly popped popcorn

FOR THE TOPPING
★ 100 g/4 oz peeled prawns, thawed if frozen
★ grated rind and juice of ^{1}/$_2$ lemon
★ 4 spring onions, trimmed and finely chopped
★ 1 eating apple, cored and finely chopped
★ salt and freshly ground black pepper
★ 200 g/7 oz fromage frais
★ 15 ml/1 tbsp tomato purée

Pop the popcorn in a large heavy-based pan as previously described, just before required.

Drain the prawns thoroughly and gently squeeze out any excess moisture using kitchen paper. Finely chop and place in a mixing bowl.

Add the lemon rind and juice, the spring onions and apple. Season to taste.

Blend the fromage frais with the tomato purée then stir into the prawn mixture.

Mix together well, then place on top of the freshly popped popcorn and serve immediately.

HICKORY DICKORY

**TRY SERVING THIS AT A DRINKS PARTY WITH
A SELECTION OF OTHER NIBBLES. IT IS GUARANTEED TO BE EATEN FIRST.**

★ 1 L/1³/₄ pts freshly popped
popcorn

FOR THE MIX

★ 15 ml/1 tbsp sunflower or
corn oil

★ 50 g/2 oz whole walnuts or
pecan nuts

★ 7.5-15 g/¹/₂-1 tbsp hickory
seasoning

Pop the popcorn in a large heavy-based pan as previously described, just before required.

Heat the oil in a large heavy-based pan then sauté the nuts for 3 minutes, stirring frequently. Remove from the heat. Add the freshly popped popcorn and hickory seasoning and cover with a tight-fitting lid.

Shake gently until the popcorn is completely coated and place into small bowls. Serve.

26

kids' treats

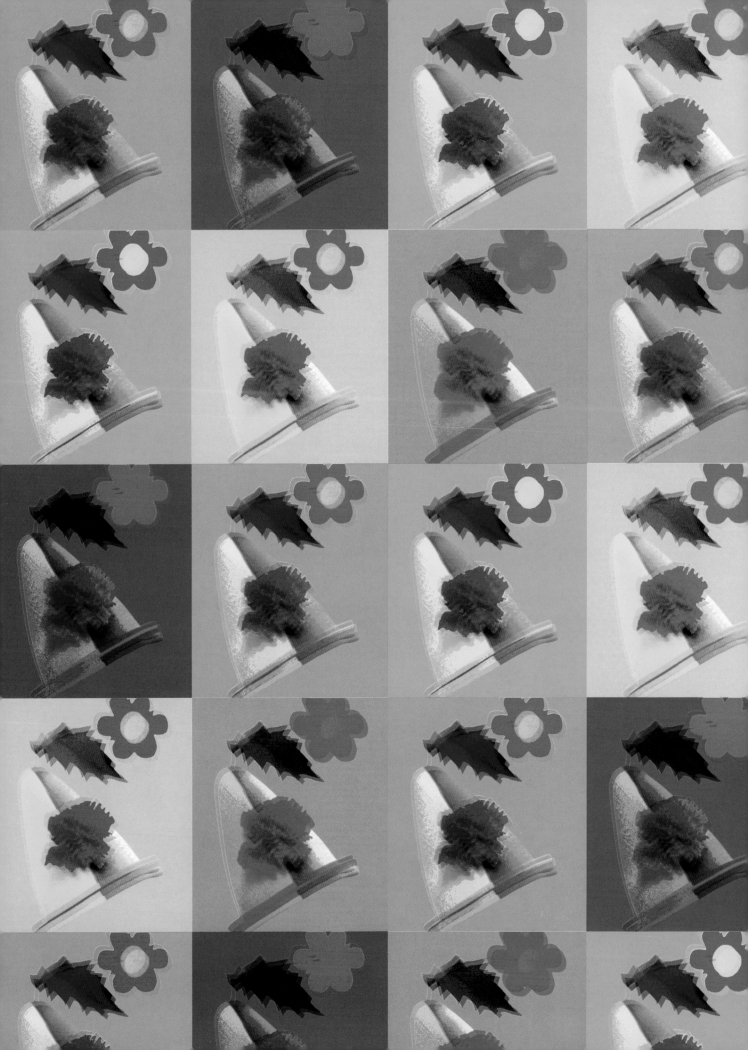

Chapter Two
2

sophisticated
savouries

Italian Style Topping

Ideal for serving as a pre-dinner appetizer.

- ★ 1 L/1^3/$_4$ pts freshly popped popcorn

FOR THE TOPPING
- ★ 45 ml/3 tbsp sunflower oil or reserved oil from the sun-dried tomatoes
- ★ 25 g/1 oz butter
- ★ 8 sun-dried tomatoes in oil, drained and finely chopped

- ★ pinch of salt
- ★ 2.5 g/^{1}/$_2$ tsp freshly ground black pepper
- ★ 30 ml/2 tbsp lemon juice
- ★ 50 g/2 oz/^{1}/$_2$ cup Parmesan cheese, grated
- ★ 30 g/2 tbsp basil, freshly chopped

Pop the popcorn in a large heavy-based pan as previously described, just before required.

Melt the butter and oil in a pan then add the sun-dried tomatoes. Sauté gently for 5 minutes or until the tomatoes are soft, stirring occasionally.

Add the seasoning together with the lemon juice, Parmesan cheese and basil and stir well. Remove from the heat and cool.

Add the freshly popped popcorn to the pan, cover with a tight-fitting lid and shake gently or stir gently with a wooden spoon until the popcorn is completely coated.

Place in a large serving bowl and serve.

30

COOL SALSA

**SERVE THIS POPCORN AS A SNACK WITH
TEQUILAS ON WARM SUMMER EVENINGS WHEN FRIENDS
HAVE POPPED ROUND.**

★ 1 l/1³/₄ pts freshly popped popcorn

FOR THE TOPPING
★ 1 small red pepper, deseeded, blanched and chopped
★ 2 ripe tomatoes, deseeded, peeled and finely chopped
★ 5 cm/2 in piece cucumber, peeled and finely chopped

★ 4 spring onions, trimmed and finely chopped
★ grated rind and juice of 2 limes
★ 30 g/2 tbsp coriander, freshly chopped
★ salt and freshly ground black pepper
★ celery sticks or taco chips, to serve

Pop the popcorn in a large heavy-based pan as previously described, just before required.

Place the red pepper, tomatoes, cucumber and spring onions in a mixing bowl.

Stir in the lime rind and juice together with the coriander.

Season to taste, then place in a small mixing bowl, cover and leave for 30 minutes in the refrigerator for the flavours to develop.

Turn the freshly popped popcorn into a bowl. Spoon on the topping and stir gently. Serve with sticks of celery or taco chips for scooping.

31

CARIBBEAN DREAM TOPPING

SERVE WITH A FEW GLASSES OF MALIBU – THEN RELAX, LIE BACK AND ENJOY THE SUN.

★ 1 L/1$^3/_4$ pts freshly popped popcorn

FOR THE TOPPING
★ 1 small ripe papaya, deseeded, peeled and finely chopped
★ 30 ml/2 tbsp lime juice
★ 15 g/1 tbsp molasses sugar
★ salt and cayenne pepper
★ 1-2 Scotch bonnet chilli peppers, deseeded and finely chopped
★ or 5 g/1 tsp chilli peppers, freshly minced
★ 50 g/2 oz freshly shaved coconut flesh or flakes
★ 15 g/1 tbsp mint, freshly chopped

Pop the popcorn in a large heavy-based pan as previously described, just before required.

Place the chopped papaya together with the lime juice, molasses sugar, seasoning, the chopped or minced chillies and the coconut flesh in a large mixing bowl.

Add the chopped mint and stir the mixture well.

Add the freshly popped popcorn to the bowl and stir gently with a wooden spoon until the popcorn is completely coated. Serve immediately.

TAPAS-STYLE POPCORN

SERVED WITH A VARIETY OF OTHER TAPAS-STYLE DISHES, THIS DISH WILL BE AN INSTANT HIT WITH ALL.

★ 1 L/1$^3/_4$ pts freshly popped popcorn

FOR THE TOPPING
★ 45 ml/3 tbsp olive oil
★ $^1/_2$ Spanish onion, chopped
★ 2 cloves of garlic, crushed
★ 1 small yellow pepper, deseeded and finely chopped
★ 75 g/3 oz chorizo sausage
★ 1 x 50 g/2 oz can anchovy fillets, drained and chopped
★ 50 g/2 oz black olives, pitted and roughly chopped
★ salt and freshly ground black pepper
★ 30 g/2 tbsp parsley, freshly chopped

Pop the popcorn in a large heavy-based pan as previously described, just before required.

Heat the oil in a large pan and gently sauté the onion and garlic for 5 minutes. Add the pepper and continue to sauté for a further 3 minutes.

Chop the chorizo sausage into small cubes then add to the pan together with the anchovies and chopped olives. Season to taste then stir in the parsley. Heat through for 2 to 3 minutes, stirring occasionally.

Place the freshly popped popcorn into small serving bowls then add the prepared topping to each. Serve immediately with chunks of bread.

CREAMY-BLUE CHEESY TOPPING

THERE ARE MANY VARIETIES OF BLUE CHEESE AVAILABLE, SOME CREAMY AND MILD, SOME STRONG AND CRUMBLY. TRY VARYING THE TYPE OF BLUE CHEESE IN THIS TOPPING TO GIVE A DIFFERENT FLAVOUR AND TEXTURE.

★ 1 L/1$\frac{3}{4}$ pts freshly popped popcorn

FOR THE TOPPING
★ 75 g/3 oz Roquefort cheese, crumbled
★ 30-45 ml/2-3 tbsp crème fraîche
★ 2 celery sticks, trimmed and finely chopped
★ 1 small onion, peeled and grated
★ 50 g/2 oz walnuts, finely chopped

Pop the popcorn in a large heavy-based pan as previously described, just before required.

Place the cheese in a heavy-based pan with the crème fraîche and heat gently, stirring continuously until the cheese has melted.

Add the celery and onion and continue to heat gently for 1 to 2 minutes.

Stir in the walnuts and remove from the heat and cool. Add the freshly popped popcorn and stir gently until the popcorn is completely coated. Serve immediately and eat with forks.

FRENCH-STYLE MIX

IF YOU LOVE GARLIC, THEN YOU'LL LOVE THIS MIX. FOR AN EXTRA SPECIAL TREAT, LOOK OUT FOR SMOKED GARLIC AND USE IT IN PLACE OF ORDINARY GARLIC.

★ 1 L/1$\frac{3}{4}$ pts freshly popped popcorn

FOR THE MIX
★ 3-4 cloves of garlic
★ 45 ml/3 tbsp virgin olive oil
★ 15 g/1 tbsp lemon rind, freshly grated
★ pinch of salt
★ 15 g/1 tbsp parsley, freshly chopped

Pop the popcorn in a large heavy-based pan as previously described, just before required.

Peel the garlic and either chop very finely or crush. Heat the olive oil in a large pan then gently sauté the garlic for 2 minutes, stirring frequently.

Add the lemon rind, salt and parsley and heat through gently for a further 1 minute, stirring occasionally. Remove the pan from the heat and allow to cool. Add the freshly popped popcorn to the pan and cover with a tight-fitting lid. Shake vigorously – or stir with a wooden spoon until the popcorn is completely coated.

Place in individual serving bowls and eat on the same day.

33

FIERY MEXICAN

THIS POPCORN IS FUN TO SERVE AS AN HORS D'OEUVRE IN PLACE OF A MORE TRADITIONAL RECIPE. REMEMBER TO TAKE GREAT CARE WHEN HANDLING RAW CHILLIES.

* 1 L/1$^{3}/_{4}$ pts freshly popped popcorn

FOR THE TOPPING
* 1 red pepper
* 45 ml/3 tbsp sunflower or corn oil
* 2-3 habanero red chilli peppers, deseeded and finely chopped
* 1 small onion, peeled and chopped

* 2 cloves of garlic, peeled and crushed
* 1 small ripe, firm avocado
* grated rind and juice of $^{1}/_{2}$ lemon
* 30 g/2 tbsp flat-leaf parsley, freshly chopped
* salt and freshly ground black pepper

Pop the popcorn in a large heavy-based pan as previously described, just before required.

Pre-heat the grill and cut the red pepper in half and discard the seeds. Place skin-side uppermost on the grill rack sitting in the grill pan. Pour over 30 ml/2 tbsp of the oil then cook, for about 10 minutes or until the skins have blistered and blackened. Take care not to burn the pepper. Remove from the heat and allow to cool before peeling. Discard the skin and chop into strips and reserve until needed.

Heat the remaining oil in a pan then sauté the chopped chillies, onion and garlic for 5 minutes, stirring occasionally.

Add the chopped pepper and continue to heat through for a further 1 minute.

Peel the avocado and discard the stone. Chop the flesh into small dice and toss in the lemon juice.

Add to the pan with the lemon rind and herbs and season to taste. Heat through, stirring occasionally for 2 to 3 minutes or until hot.

Place the freshly popped popcorn in a serving bowl. Top with the chilli and avocado topping and serve immediately.

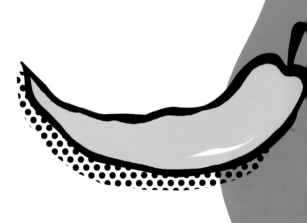

'COOL MON'

JAMAICAN HOT PEPPER SAUCE IS GROWING IN
POPULARITY. IF USING FOR THE FIRST TIME, TAKE CARE; IT'S A SERIOUSLY HOT
SAUCE AND IS CERTAINLY NOT INTENDED FOR THE FAINT-HEARTED.

★ 1 L/1$\frac{3}{4}$ pts freshly popped
popcorn

FOR THE MIX
★ 3 tbsp/40 g/1$\frac{1}{2}$ oz butter
★ pinch of salt
★ 30 g/2 tbsp paprika pepper
★ few shakes of Jamaican Hot
Pepper sauce, to taste

Pop the popcorn in a large heavy-based pan as previously described, just before required.

Melt the butter in a large pan and remove from the heat. Add the salt, paprika pepper, Hot Pepper sauce and the freshly popped popcorn.

Cover the pan with a tight-fitting lid and shake vigorously for 1 minute or stir with a wooden spoon until the popcorn is completely coated. Serve warm or cold.

36

HOT'N'SPICY

TRY THIS TOPPING OVER POPCORN AT THE START OF AN INDIAN MEAL WITH SOME LONG COOL BEERS.

★ 1 L/1^3/$_4$ pts freshly popped popcorn

FOR THE TOPPING

★ 30 ml/2 tbsp sunflower or corn oil
★ 1 onion, peeled and finely chopped
★ 2 cloves of garlic, peeled and crushed
★ 2-3 green chilli peppers, deseeded and chopped

★ 10 g/2 tsp root ginger, freshly minced
★ 5 g/1 tsp ground coriander
★ 5 g/1 tsp ground cumin
★ 5 g/1 tsp ground cinnamon
★ 5 g/1 tsp fenugreek seeds, crushed
★ 2.5 g/^{1}/$_2$ tsp turmeric
★ 150 ml/^{1}/$_4$ pt natural yoghurt
★ 30 g/2 tbps coriander leaves, to garnish

Pop the popcorn in a large heavy-based pan as previously described, just before required.

Heat the oil in a frying pan then sauté the onion, garlic and chillies for 3 minutes.

Add the ginger and spices and continue to sauté for 3 more minutes over a gentle heat, stirring occasionally. Stir in the yoghurt and cook for 2 to 3 minutes, stirring frequently.

Sprinkle with the coriander and mix well. Remove from the heat and allow to cool.

SAUCY TAVERNA POPCORN

ZORBA WOULD NEVER HAVE STOPPED DANCING IF HE HAD EATEN A FEW BOWLS OF THIS!

★ 1 L/1³/₄ pts freshly popped popcorn

FOR THE TOPPING

★ 1 red onion, peeled and sliced

★ 100 g/4 oz feta cheese, cut into cubes

★ 2 tomatoes, peeled and sliced

★ 50 g/2 oz pitted, whole black olives

★ 150 ml/¹/₄ pt Greek style yoghurt

★ 15 g/1 tbsp mint, freshly chopped

★ warm pitta bread, to serve

Pop the popcorn in a large heavy-based pan as previously described, just before required.

Place the onion in a mixing bowl together with the feta cheese, tomatoes and olives.

Stir in the yoghurt and mint. Mix together well. Place the freshly popped popcorn into a serving dish and spoon over the topping. Stir gently until the popcorn is completely coated.

Serve immediately with warm pitta bread cut into strips to use as scoops.

38

FRAGRANT MIX

WARM SAKI IS A MUST TO SERVE WITH THESE LITTLE MORSELS.

★ 1 L/1³/₄ pts freshly popped popcorn

FOR THE MIX
★ 3 lemon grass stalks
★ 1 Thai red chilli pepper, deseeded
★ 45 ml/3 tbsp sunflower or corn oil
★ 5 g/1 tsp root ginger, freshly minced
★ 15 ml/1 tbsp soy sauce
★ 15 ml/1 tbsp lime juice
★ 50 g/2 oz fresh coconut flesh, grated

Pop the popcorn in a large heavy-based pan as previously described, just before required.

Remove the outer leaves from the lemon grass and chop the lemon grass and chilli very finely.

Heat the oil in a medium-sized pan then gently sauté the lemon grass, chilli, and ginger for 3 minutes, stirring frequently.

Add the soy sauce and lime juice and cook for a further 30 seconds. Remove from the heat and allow to cool slightly. Add the freshly popped popcorn and coconut and cover with a tight-fitting lid. Shake or stir gently with a wooden spoon until the popcorn is completely coated. Eat warm or cold.

MADRAS-STYLE POPCORN

DON'T BE TEMPTED TO CHEAT AND JUST USE CURRY POWDER, THE FLAVOUR JUST WON'T BE THE SAME.

★ 1 L/1³/₄ pts freshly popped popcorn

FOR THE MIX
★ 30 ml/2 tbsp sunflower or corn oil
★ 2 cloves of garlic, peeled and crushed
★ 1-2 Thai chilli peppers, deseeded and chopped
★ 5-10 g/1-2 tsp chilli powder
★ 15 g/3 tsp garam masala
★ 15 ml/1 tbsp tomato purée
★ 15 ml/1 tbsp lemon juice

Pop the popcorn in a large, heavy-based pan as previously described, just before required.

Heat the oil in a large pan then sauté the garlic and the chillies for 3 minutes.

Add the chilli powder and garam masala and continue to sauté gently for a further 3 minutes, stirring frequently.

Blend the tomato purée with the lemon juice and stir into the spice mix. Cook for 30 seconds. Remove the pan from the heat and allow to cool slightly.

Add the freshly popped popcorn, cover with a tight-fitting lid and shake or stir gently with a wooden spoon until the popcorn is completely coated with the mix.

40

TRAIL MIX

**IF YOU'RE WATCHING YOUR CALORIES,
TRY THIS HEALTHY ALTERNATIVE TO THE BUTTERY OR SWEET TOPPINGS.**

★ 1 L/1^3/$_4$ pts freshly popped
popcorn

FOR THE MIX
★ grated rind of 2 oranges
★ 50 g/2 oz no-need-to-soak
apricots, finely chopped
★ 50 g/2 oz no-need-to-soak
prunes, finely chopped
★ 50 g/2 oz toasted sesame seeds
★ 50 g/2 oz toasted pumpkin
seeds

Pop the popcorn in a large heavy-based pan as previously described, then while still in the pan, add the grated orange rind. Cover with a tight-fitting lid and shake vigorously until the popcorn is completely coated with the rind.

Add the remaining ingredients to the freshly popped popcorn and mix together well. Eat the same day.

NUTTY TREASURE MIX

**SQUIRRELS WON'T BE THE ONLY LOVERS
OF THESE NIBBLES. KIDS OF ALL AGES WILL GO "NUTS"
OVER THIS POPCORN!**

★ 1 L/1³/₄ pts freshly popped popcorn

FOR THE MIX
★ 30 ml/2 tbsp olive oil
★ 50 g/2 oz pine kernels

★ 50 g/2 oz pecan nuts, roughly chopped
★ 75 g/3 oz candied pineapple, chopped
★ 50 g/2 oz dried coconut flakes

Pop the popcorn in a large heavy-based pan as previously described, just before required.

Heat the oil in a pan then gently sauté the pine kernels for 2 to 3 minutes or until lightly toasted. Add the chopped pecan nuts for the last minute.

Remove from the heat and stir in the remaining ingredients except the freshly popped popcorn. Cool slightly then add the popcorn. Stir gently with a wooden spoon to ensure that the ingredients are well mixed. Eat the same day or store in airtight containers.

42

PESTO SURPRISE

YOU CAN USE A PESTLE AND MORTAR TO MAKE THE PESTO IF PREFERRED. HOWEVER, WHICHEVER WAY YOU CHOOSE, EAT ON THE SAME DAY.

★ 1 L/1³/₄ pts freshly popped popcorn

FOR THE MIX
★ 15 g/1 tbsp fresh basil leaves
★ 1 clove of garlic, peeled and crushed

★ 25 g/1 oz pine kernels
★ 60 ml/4 tbsp olive oil
★ 1 tbsp/15 g/¹/₂ oz freshly grated Parmesan cheese
★ pinch of salt
★ freshly shaved Parmesan, to garnish

Pop the popcorn in a large heavy-based pan as previously described, just before required.

Place the basil, garlic and pine kernels in a food processor then blend to form a purée slowly pouring in the oil while the machine is still running.

Place the purée in a bowl and stir in the cheese and salt.

Allow the freshly popped popcorn to cool in the pan then add the pesto sauce.

Stir gently with a wooden spoon to coat popcorn. Add Parmesan shavings and serve.

Chapter Three

sweet ideas

CHOCOHOLICS

**IF YOU'RE A CHOCOHOLIC,
THEN THIS FUN-FLAVOURED POPCORN IS A
MUST FOR YOU.**

★ 1 L/1$^3/_4$ pts freshly popped popcorn

FOR THE MIX
★ 100 g/4 oz plain chocolate
★ 2 tbsp/25 g/1 oz butter
★ 45 ml/3 tbsp golden syrup

Pop the popcorn in a large heavy-based pan as previously described, just before required.

Break the chocolate into small pieces then place in a large heavy-based pan together with the butter and syrup.

Place over a gentle heat and allow the mixture to melt, stirring occasionally with a wooden spoon.

When the chocolate has melted, bring to the boil and boil steadily for 1 minute.

Remove from the heat and add the freshly popped popcorn, stirring gently with a wooden spoon until the popcorn is completely coated and allow to cool. Eat the same day.

If desired, sprinkle with grated white chocolate.

46

SMOOTHIE FRUITY POPS

**IF PEANUT BUTTER IS YOUR FORTE,
YOU'LL LOVE THIS MIX. LOOK OUT FOR JARS OF PEANUT BUTTER AND
JELLY IN YOUR LOCAL SUPERMARKET.**

★ 1 L/1³/₄ pts freshly popped popcorn

FOR THE MIX

★ 2 tbsp/25 g/1 oz smooth peanut butter with jelly

★ 45 ml/3 tbsp golden syrup

★ 75 g/3 oz no-need-to-soak prunes, finely chopped

★ 30-45 ml/2-3 tbsp double cream

Pop the popcorn in a large heavy-based pan as previously described, just before required.

Place the peanut butter with jelly and the syrup in a large pan and heat gently until melted, stirring occasionally.

Bring to the boil and simmer for 1 minute then remove from the heat and stir in the prunes and cream. Return to the heat and heat for a further 30 seconds, stirring continuously. Remove from the heat again and leave to cool for about 1 minute.

Add the freshly popped popcorn and stir until it is completely coated.

Turn into a serving dish and serve. Eat the same day.

48

MALLOW DELIGHT

IDEAL FOR THOSE WITH A SWEET AND FRUITY PALATE.

★ 1 L/1$^3/_4$ pts freshly popped popcorn

FOR THE MIX
★ 100 g/4 oz marshmallows

★ 2 tbsp/25 g/1 oz butter
★ 30 ml/2 tbsp milk
★ 50 g/2 oz glacé cherries, chopped
★ 25 g/1 oz angelica, chopped

Pop the popcorn in a large heavy-based pan as previously described, just before required.

Chop 50 g/2 oz of the marshmallows into small pieces and reserve for mixing into the popcorn with the cherries.

Place the remaining marshmallows with the butter and milk in a heavy-based pan and heat gently until the marshmallows have melted. Stir until smooth.

Add the chopped glacé cherries, remaining marshmallows and angelica and stir together well. Remove from the heat and allow to cool. Add the freshly popped popcorn and stir gently. Place in bowls and serve.

NUTTY BITES

**YOU'LL GO CRAZY FOR THIS POPCORN.
ONCE YOU START EATING IT, YOU JUST WON'T BE ABLE TO STOP –
IT'S DEFINITELY VERY, VERY MOREISH.**

★ 1 L/1³/₄ pts freshly popped popcorn

FOR THE MIX

★ 100 g/4 oz granulated sugar

★ 50 g/2 oz whole shelled pistachio nuts

★ 50 g/2 oz almond flakes, toasted

★ a few drops of almond essence

Pop the popcorn in a large heavy-based pan as previously described, just before serving.

Melt the sugar in a heavy-based pan with 150 ml/¼ pt of water over a gentle heat. Stir occasionally then once the sugar has melted, bring to the boil and cook for 3 minutes or until a light syrup has formed.

Remove from the heat and stir in the nuts and almond essence and allow to cool slightly.

Gently stir in the freshly popped popcorn then leave to cool a little before eating.

50

YANKEE DOODLE TREAT

BRIBE THE KIDS WITH THIS DESSERT, IT WILL GUARANTEE CLEAN PLATES.

★ 1 L/1$\frac{3}{4}$ pts freshly popped popcorn

FOR THE TOPPING

★ 2 tbsp/25 g/1 oz smooth peanut butter
★ 30 ml/2 tbsp golden syrup

★ 30-45 ml/2-3 tbsp double cream
★ ice cream, to serve
★ chocolate sugar strands, to decorate

Pop the popcorn in a large heavy-based pan as previously described, just before required.

Place the peanut butter and syrup in a large heavy-based pan and heat, stirring occasionally, until the peanut butter has melted.

Bring to the boil, and simmer for 1 minute, then stir in the cream. Cook for 30 seconds, and remove from the heat. Cool slightly, then add the freshly popped popcorn and stir gently with a wooden spoon until completely coated.

Place scoops of ice cream in serving bowls, top with the peanut butter popcorn and serve sprinkled with chocolate sugar strands.

MOCHA MAGIC

IF YOU LOVE CAPPUCCINO, THIS POPCORN IS A MUST.

★ 1 L/1^3/$_4$ pts freshly popped popcorn

FOR THE MIX
★ 75 g/3 oz plain chocolate
★ 15 ml/1 tbsp very strong black coffee
★ 1 tbsp/15 g/^{1}/$_2$ oz butter
★ 30 ml/2 tbsp double cream
★ 10 g/2 tsp cocoa powder, sifted

Pop the popcorn in a large heavy-based pan as previously described, just before required.

Break the chocolate into a large heavy-based pan and add the coffee and butter.

Melt over a gentle heat, stirring occasionally until smooth. Add the cream and continue to cook gently for a further 1 minute.

Remove from the heat, allow to cool slightly and gently stir in the freshly popped popcorn. Keep stirring until the popcorn is completely coated.

Remove from the heat and place in serving containers. Serve sprinkled with the sifted cocoa powder.

TOFFEE POPS

KIDS WILL LOVE THIS POPCORN AND IT WILL BECOME A BIG HIT AT PARTIES OR WHEN THEY RETURN HOME FROM SCHOOL.

★ 1 L/1^3/$_4$ pts freshly popped popcorn

FOR THE MIX
★ 2 tbsp/25 g/1 oz butter
★ 30 ml/2 tbsp golden syrup
★ 50 g/2 oz dark soft brown sugar
★ 50 ml/2 fl oz double cream

Pop the popcorn in a large heavy-based pan as previously described, just before required.

Melt the butter, syrup and sugar in a large heavy-based pan over a gentle heat, stirring occasionally with a wooden spoon until blended.

Add the cream, stirring all the time, then bring to the boil and remove from the heat just as it reaches boiling point.

Cool slightly then add the freshly popped popcorn and stir gently until completely coated. Serve warm or cold.

53

SYRUPY AFTERTHOUGHTS

TRY PUTTING SMALL SPOONFULS INTO PETITS FOURS CASES AND SERVING AFTER DESSERT. JUST WATCH THE FAMILY'S EYES LIGHT UP.

★ 1 L/1$^{3}/_{4}$ pts freshly popped popcorn

FOR THE MIX

★ 60 ml/4 tbsp golden syrup

★ 2 tbsp/25 g/1 oz butter

★ 15 g/1 tbsp cocoa powder, sifted

★ a few drops of vanilla essence

★ 75 g/3 oz pecan nuts, roughly chopped

Pop the popcorn in a large heavy-based pan as previously described, just before required.

Melt the syrup, butter and cocoa powder in a heavy-based pan over a gentle heat, stirring occasionally with a wooden spoon until blended.

When the syrup has melted, bring to the boil and cook for 1 minute then remove from the heat and stir in the vanilla essence and nuts.

Allow to cool slightly, then stir in the freshly popped popcorn. Stir gently until the popcorn is completely coated then place in containers or bowls. Eat on the same day.

54

SHOOFLY PUFF

**COME DOWN TO THE DEEP SOUTH AND
GET A TASTE OF SHEER HEAVEN.**

★ 1 L/1³/₄ pts freshly popped
  popcorn

FOR THE MIX
★ 75 g/3 oz molasses sugar
★ 2 tbsp/25 g/1 oz butter

★ 10 g/1 tsp ground cinnamon
★ 2.5 g/¹/₂ tsp freshly grated
  nutmeg
★ 2.5 g/¹/₂ tsp ground ginger
★ 45 ml/3 tbsp double cream

Pop the popcorn in a large
heavy-based pan as previously
described, just before required.

Place the sugar, butter and
spices in a large heavy-based
pan and heat gently, stirring
frequently until the sugar and
butter have melted.

Add the cream and stir well then
bring to just below boiling point.
Remove from the heat and allow
to cool slightly. Add the freshly
popped popcorn and stir well
until it is completely coated.
Spoon into serving bowls and
eat the same day.

MINTY POPS

**SERVE THIS FUN-FLAVORED
POPCORN AFTER DINNER AS A DIFFERENT KIND
OF PETITS FOURS.**

★ 1 L/1³/₄ pts freshly popped popcorn

FOR THE MIX

★ 75 g/3 oz granulated sugar

★ 30 ml/2 tbsp crème de menthe
★ 50 g/2 oz crème de menthe-flavoured Turkish delight

Pop the popcorn in a large heavy-based pan as previously described, just before required.

Melt the sugar with 150 ml/¼ pt of water in a large heavy-based pan. Bring to the boil and boil steadily for 3 minutes or until a light sugar syrup has formed.

Remove from the heat and stir in the crème de menthe and allow to cool slightly.

Chop the crème de menthe-flavoured Turkish delight into small pieces then add to the pan together with the freshly popped popcorn. Stir gently until completely coated.

Place in small serving dishes and eat on the same day.

BOOZY CHOCS

**FOR SERIOUS DEVOTEES
OF POPCORN AND CHOCOLATE.**

★ 1 L/1³/₄ pts freshly popped popcorn

FOR THE MIX

★ 100 g/4 oz plain dark chocolate

★ 2 tbsp/25 g/1 oz butter
★ 30 ml/2 tbsp single cream
★ 50 g/2 oz raisins
★ 30 ml/2 tbsp rum

Pop the popcorn in a large heavy-based pan as previously described, just before required.

Break the chocolate into small pieces and place in a large heavy-based pan together with the butter and single cream. Melt over a gentle heat, stirring occasionally until smooth. Once

melted, cook for 1 minute. Remove from the heat. Add the raisins and rum and stir well. Allow to cool slightly. Add the freshly popped popcorn and stir until completely coated.

Place in serving bowls and eat on the same day.

56

★ 57

GINGERED CRISP

**PEP UP YOUR PALATE WITH
THIS CRUNCHY TOPPING.**

★ 1 L/1³/₄ pts freshly popped
   popcorn

FOR THE MIX

★ 100 g/4 oz ginger nut biscuits

★ 2 tbsp/25 g/1 oz butter
★ 45 ml/3 tbsp golden syrup
★ 25 g/1 oz stem ginger, chopped

Pop the popcorn in a large
heavy-based pan as previously
described, just before required.

Roughly crush the biscuits into
bite-sized pieces and reserve.

Heat the butter and syrup in a
heavy-based pan then stir
continuously until melted.
Remove from the heat, allow to
cool slightly then stir in the
crushed biscuits and freshly
popped popcorn. Stir gently
with a wooden spoon taking
care not to crush the biscuits
any more. Sprinkle with the stem
ginger. Eat the same day.

Chapter Four

fruity afterthoughts

APRICOT MELBA

A VERY ORIGINAL VERSION OF THE CLASSIC DISH THAT IS UNIVERSALLY POPULAR. THIS ONE WILL BECOME EVEN MORE POPULAR.

★ 1 L/1^3/$_4$ pts freshly popped popcorn

FOR THE TOPPING
★ 350 g/12 oz fresh raspberries
★ 15 ml/1 tbsp lemon juice

★ 4-4^1/$_2$ tbsp/25-50 g/1-2 oz icing sugar or to taste, sifted
★ 10 g/2 tsp arrowroot
★ 50-75 g/2-3 oz no-need-to-soak dried apricots

Pop the popcorn in a large heavy-based pan as previously described, just before required.

Pick over the raspberries and place in a blender together with the lemon juice and sugar and blend to form a smooth purée. Pass through a fine sieve to remove the pips then place in a pan and bring to the boil.

Blend the arrowroot to a smooth paste with 30 ml/2 tbsp of water then stir into the raspberry purée. Cook, stirring for 2 to 3 minutes or until the purée has thickened. Remove from the heat and allow the purée to cool slightly.

Chop the apricots into small pieces then stir into the raspberry purée together with the freshly popped popcorn. Stir until lightly coated. Eat the same day.

60

CALYPSO

TRY A TRUE TASTE OF THE CARIBBEAN WITH THIS FRUITY MANGO TOPPING. SERVE AS A TOPPING FOR ICE CREAM.

★ 1 L/1$^3/_4$ pts freshly popped popcorn

FOR THE TOPPING

★ 1 ripe mango, peeled, stone removed and finely chopped

★ 1 small fresh pineapple, skinned, cored and finely diced

★ grated rind of 1 lime

★ 15-30 ml/1-2 tbsp clear honey, warmed

★ 50 g/2 oz coconut flakes

★ 50 g/2 oz roasted cashew nuts

Pop the popcorn in a large heavy-based pan as previously described, just before required.

Place the chopped mango flesh, pineapple, lime rind, honey, coconut flakes and cashew nuts in a large mixing bowl. Mix in the freshly popped popcorn and stir gently with a wooden spoon until lightly coated.

Place in a serving dish lined with pineapple leaves and serve.

61

TASTE OF THE TROPICS

**YOU CAN VARY THE DRIED AND GLACÉ FRUITS
USED IN THIS TOPPING ACCORDING TO YOUR OWN PERSONAL
TASTE AND AVAILABILITY OF THE FRUITS.**

★ 1 L/1³/₄ pts freshly popped popcorn

FOR THE TOPPING

★ 75 g/3 oz ready-chopped dates

★ 50 g/2 oz glacé cherries, washed, dried and chopped
★ 50 g/2 oz almond flakes, toasted
★ 50 g/2 oz sultanas

★ 50 g/2 oz banana chips
★ 45 ml/3 tbsp golden syrup
★ 2 tbsp/25 g/1 oz butter, melted

Place the dates, cherries, sultanas, almonds and banana chips together in a mixing bowl and reserve.

Pop the popcorn in a large heavy-based pan as previously described, then once the popcorn has finished popping, add the syrup and butter. Cover the pan with a tight-fitting lid and shake the pan or stir gently until the popcorn is completely coated.

Add the reserved fruit mixture and either cover and shake the pan or stir gently with a wooden spoon until the fruit mixture is evenly distributed throughout.

Serve and eat on the same day.

62

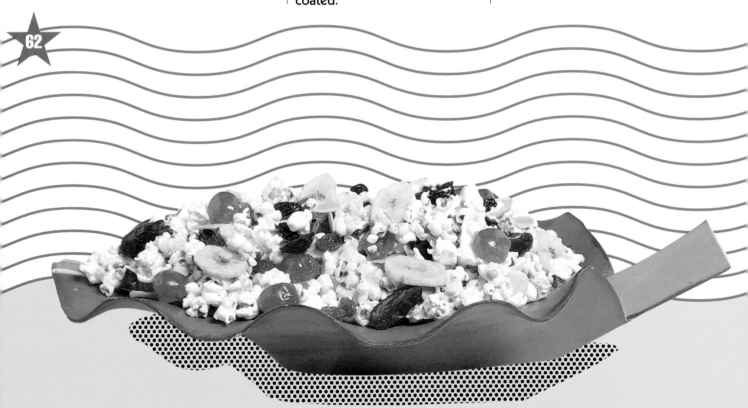

TANGY LEMON MERINGUE

**WHEN MAKING MERINGUE, IT IS ALWAYS
A GOOD IDEA TO MAKE A LITTLE EXTRA SO THAT IT CAN BE USED TO MAKE
LITTLE TINY MERINGUES WHICH ARE IDEAL AS ACCOMPANIMENTS FOR
FRUIT DESSERTS, ICE CREAM OR WITH THIS TOPPING.**

★ 1 L/1^3/$_4$ pts freshly popped popcorn

FOR THE TOPPING

★ 50 g/2 oz prepared meringues
★ grated rind and juice of 1 large lemon

★ 2 tbsp/25 g/1 oz sugar or to taste
★ 15 g/1 tbsp cornflour
★ 10 g/2 tsp butter

Pop the popcorn in a large heavy-based pan as previously described, just before required.

Crush the meringues lightly or break into pieces and reserve.

Place the lemon rind and juice made up to 120 ml/4 fl oz with water in a large pan with the sugar. Bring to the boil, stirring occasionally.

Blend the cornflour to a smooth paste with 30 ml/2 tbsp of water then stir into the boiling liquid. Cook, stirring throughout for 2 minutes, or until thickened.

Remove from the heat and add the butter, stirring until melted. Allow to cool slightly, then add the freshly popped popcorn and crushed meringues. Stir gently until the popcorn and meringues are completely coated then serve.

63

CHIP CHOC

LOOK OUT FOR DIFFERENT FLAVORED CHOCOLATE CHIPS. THEY ARE AVAILABLE IN DARK, MILK AND WHITE.

★ 1 L/1^3/$_4$ pts freshly popped popcorn

FOR THE MIX
★ 40 g/1^1/$_2$ oz plain chocolate chips
★ 40 g/1^1/$_2$ oz milk chocolate chips
★ 25 g/1 oz white chocolate chips
★ 50 g/2 oz dried banana chips
★ 45 ml/3 tbsp golden syrup

Place all the chocolate and banana chips in a mixing bowl and reserve.

Cook the popcorn in a large heavy-based pan as previously described and once the corn has finished popping, add the syrup.

Heat through for 1 minute and cover the pan with a tight-fitting lid. Shake vigorously, or stir with a wooden spoon.

Add the reserved chocolate chips and banana chips and mix lightly. Eat on the same day of making.

64

KEY LIME

A VARIATION OF THE FAMOUS KEY LIME PIE THAT ORIGINATED FROM KEY WEST IN FLORIDA, THIS ONE HOWEVER CAN BE NIBBLED ANY TIME, DAY OR NIGHT.

★ 1 L/1^3/$_4$ pts freshly popped popcorn

FOR THE MIX
★ 150 ml/^{1}/$_4$ pt condensed milk
★ 2 tbsp/25 g/1 oz butter
★ juice and grated rind of 2 limes
★ 50 g/2 oz prepared meringues, lightly crushed

Pop the popcorn in a large heavy-based pan as previously described, just before required.

Place the condensed milk and butter in a heavy-based pan. Bring to the boil, stirring frequently, then reduce the heat and simmer gently for 5 minutes, again stirring frequently. Remove from the heat and stir in the lime juice and rind. Allow to cool slightly then stir in the freshly popped popcorn and lightly crushed meringue.

Stir gently until completely coated then leave until cold before eating.

REDCURRANT AND PORT

SERVE THIS POPCORN AT CHRISTMAS TIME AS AN APPETIZER TO THE CHRISTMAS MEAL, BUT ENSURE YOUR GUESTS DON'T EAT SO MUCH OF THE POPCORN THAT THEY HAVE NO ROOM FOR THE TURKEY.

★ 1 L/1^3/$_4$ pts freshly popped popcorn

FOR THE MIX
★ 45 g/3 tbsp redcurrant jelly
★ 15 ml/1 tbsp orange juice
★ grated rind of 1 small orange
★ 15-30 ml/1-2 tbsp port
★ 15 ml/1 tbsp mint, freshly chopped

Pop the popcorn in a large heavy-based pan as previously described, just before required.

Heat the redcurrant jelly in a large pan with the orange juice and rind, stirring frequently with a wooden spoon until smooth.

Bring to the boil and boil for 1 minute. Remove from the heat and stir in the port and mint. Remove from the heat and allow to cool slightly.

Add the freshly popped popcorn to the pan.

Stir gently with a wooden spoon until the popcorn is lightly coated. Allow to cool before serving in small bowls.

APRICOT AND ALMOND DELIGHTS

USE THE BEST QUALITY CONSERVE YOU CAN BUY FOR THIS RECIPE. YOU CERTAINLY WON'T REGRET IT.

★ 1 L/1^3/$_4$ pts freshly popped popcorn

FOR THE MIX
★ 60 g/4 tbsp apricot conserve
★ a few drops of almond essence
★ 15 ml/1 tbsp lemon juice
★ 50 g/2 oz whole blanched almonds, cut into slivers

Pop the popcorn in a large heavy-based pan as previously described, just before required.

If the conserve has large pieces of fruit in it, chop into bite-sized pieces then place the conserve with the lemon juice and almond essence in a large pan.

Heat through gently, stirring occasionally until smooth. Remove from the heat and allow to cool slightly.

Add the slivered almonds and freshly popped popcorn and stir with a wooden spoon until the popcorn is completely coated.

Place in serving bowls and eat on the same day. If desired, some chopped no-need-to-soak apricots can be added as well for an extra fruity snack.

65

BRANDIED CHOCOLATE CHERRY CORN

LOOK OUT FOR THE NATURAL GLACÉ CHERRIES WHEN MAKING THIS. WASH AND DRY THE CHERRIES THOROUGHLY BEFORE ADDING TO THE MIX.

★ 1 L/1$^3/_4$ pts freshly popped popcorn

FOR THE MIX
★ 100 g/4 oz plain chocolate
★ 2 tbsp/25 g/1 oz butter
★ 30 ml/2 tbsp brandy
★ 30 ml/2 tbsp double cream
★ 75 g/3 oz whole glacé cherries

Pop the popcorn in a large heavy-based pan as previously described, just before required.

Break the chocolate into small pieces and place in a heavy-based pan together with the butter and brandy.

Heat gently until the chocolate has melted, stirring occasionally with a wooden spoon. Remove from the heat and stir in the double cream.

Add the freshly popped popcorn and the cherries. Stir until the popcorn is completely coated. Leave to cool before serving. Eat on the same day.

66

HONEY KISSES

THERE ARE MANY VARIETIES OF HONEY AVAILABLE THESE DAYS VARYING FROM FRAGRANT AND FLOWERY TO DARK RICH, SMOKEY FLAVOURS. CHOOSE ONE WITH A PRONOUNCED FLAVOUR.

★ 1 L/1$^{3}/_{4}$ pts freshly popped popcorn

FOR THE MIX

★ 60 ml/4 tbsp Mexican or similar honey

★ 2 tbsp/25 g/1 oz butter
★ 15 ml/1 tbsp golden syrup
★ 15 g/1 tbsp desiccated coconut

Pop the popcorn in a large heavy-based pan as previously described, just before required.

Pour the honey into a large pan and add the butter and syrup. Place over a gentle heat and heat through, stirring occasionally until the butter has melted. Bring to the boil and boil steadily for 1 minute. Remove from the heat, allow to cool slightly then stir in the desiccated coconut and freshly popped popcorn.

Stir until the popcorn is completely coated then place in a container. Eat on the same day of making.

68

ROCKY MOUNTAINS

**THIS POPCORN WILL BE A WINNER FOR ALL MAPLE SYRUP FANS.
ADD WHATEVER FRUIT OR NUTS YOU FANCY AND MUNCH AWAY TO YOUR
HEART'S CONTENT.**

★ 1 L/1^3/$_4$ pts freshly popped
popcorn

FOR THE MIX
★ 60 ml/4 tbsp maple syrup

★ 2 tbsp/25 g/1 oz butter
★ 50 g/2 oz whole hazelnuts,
shelled
★ 50 g/2 oz mixed cut peel

Pop the popcorn in a large
heavy-based pan as previously
described, just before required.

Pour the maple syrup into a large
pan and add the butter. Heat
through, stirring occasionally
until the syrup and butter are
blended. Bring to the boil and
boil for 1 minute.

Remove from the heat and stir in
the nuts, mixed peel and freshly
popped popcorn. Stir until the
popcorn is completely coated
then place in a container and
allow to cool before serving.

fun
reCipeS

WAKEY WAKEY

START THE DAY WITH A SMILE BY EATING THIS POPCORN MUESLI. APART FROM BEING REALLY TASTY, IT'S ALSO VERY HEALTHY.

* 350 ml/12 fl oz freshly popped popcorn
* 50 g/2 oz rolled oats
* 50 g/2 oz raisins
* 50 g/2 oz flaked almonds, toasted
* 50 g/2 oz no-need-to-soak apricots, chopped
* 2 bananas, sliced
* 50 g/2 oz seedless grapes, halved
* natural yoghurt, to serve

Mix together the freshly popped popcorn, oats, raisins, almonds and apricots. (This can be done the night before and kept in an airtight container.)

When ready to eat, add the bananas and grapes, top with the yoghurt and serve.

MAYO MAGIC

You can of course use either home-made or bought mayonnaise, whichever you prefer. Try varying the flavour of the mayonnaise by adding some grated lemon or orange rind.

★ 1 L/1³/₄ pts freshly popped popcorn

FOR THE TOPPING
★ 150 ml/¹/₄ pt prepared mayonnaise
★ 1-2 red fresno chilli peppers, deseeded and finely chopped
★ 1 carrot, peeled and grated
★ 50 g/2 oz raisins
★ 30 g/2 tbsp coriander, freshly chopped

★ salt and freshly ground black pepper

TO SERVE
★ 175 g/6 oz red cabbage, outer leaves and central core discarded, washed thoroughly and drained
★ 100 g/4 oz thinly sliced ham, formed into rolls

Pop the popcorn in a large heavy-based pan as previously described, just before required.

Place the mayonnaise in a bowl and stir in the chillies, carrot, raisins and coriander. Season to taste, and mix into the freshly popped popcorn.

Shred the red cabbage finely and arrange on a serving platter. Arrange the ham rolls around the edge. Top with the freshly popped popcorn and serve immediately.

73

POPCORN KRISPIES

These little chocolate cakes are a big hit for all kids. Make two batches as one certainly won't be enough.

MAKES ABOUT 8
★ 1 L/1³/₄ pts freshly popped popcorn
★ 45 ml/3 tbsp golden syrup
★ 75 g/3 oz milk chocolate, broken into pieces

★ 15 g/1 rounded tbsp cocoa powder, sifted
★ 2 tbsp/25 g/1 oz butter
★ 5 g/1 tsp vanilla essence

Pop the popcorn in a large heavy-based pan as previously described, just before required.

Heat the syrup, chocolate, cocoa powder and butter in a large pan, stirring occasionally.

Once the mixture has melted, stir until smooth then remove from the heat. Add the vanilla essence and freshly popped popcorn then spoon into small paper cases. Leave until cold before serving.

POPCORN BIRTHDAY CAKE

IF A FUN-SHAPED MOULD IS UNAVAILABLE, DRAW A SHAPE ONTO A PIECE OF BAKING PARCHMENT PLACED ON A BAKING SHEET. SPREAD THE PREPARED POPCORN WITHIN THE SHAPE.

- ★ 2 L/3½ pts freshly popped popcorn
- ★ 4 tbsp/50 g/2 oz crunchy peanut butter
- ★ 100 g/4 oz milk chocolate
- ★ 15 g/1 rounded tbsp cocoa powder, sifted

- ★ 90 ml/6 tbsp golden syrup
- ★ 15-30 ml/2-3 tbsp double cream
- ★ 175 g/6 oz icing sugar, sifted
- ★ glacé cherries, angelica and birthday candles, to decorate

Lightly oil a 23 cm/9 in cake tin or mould shaped in the form of a car, rabbit or similar.

Pop the popcorn in a large heavy-based pan as previously described and reserve.

Place the peanut butter, chocolate, cocoa powder and syrup in a large heavy-based pan and heat, stirring occasionally until smooth and well blended.

Bring to the boil and simmer for 1 minute then remove from the heat and stir in the cream. Heat for 30 seconds then remove from the heat.

Add the freshly popped popcorn and stir until the popcorn is completely coated. Press into the lightly-oiled tin or mould.

Leave until set then turn out onto a silver cake board. Mix the icing sugar with about 30-45 ml/2-3 tbsp hot water to form a coating consistency. Decorate the cake with the icing, the cherries and the candles.

74

FRUITS DE MER TOPPING

**SERVE THIS AS A FUN
STARTER FOR AN INFORMAL LUNCH OR SUPPER PARTY.**

★ 1 L/1³/₄ pts freshly popped popcorn

FOR THE TOPPING
★ 30 ml/2 tbsp olive oil
★ 1 small onion, peeled and chopped
★ grated rind of 1 lime
★ 1 x 170 g/7 oz can crab meat, drained and flaked

★ 15 ml/1 tbsp tomato purée
★ 1 x 50 g/2 oz can anchovy fillets, drained and chopped
★ 100 g/4 oz smoked salmon, thinly sliced
★ 45 ml/3 tbsp prepared mayonnaise
★ lime wedges and strips of rind, to garnish

Pop the popcorn in a large heavy-based pan as previously described, just before required.

Heat the oil in a pan then sauté the onion for 5 minutes or until soft. Remove from the heat.

Add the lime rind, flaked crab, tomato purée and chopped anchovy fillets and mix together.

Cut the smoked salmon into thin strips then add to the mixture together with the mayonnaise and stir together.

Place the freshly popped popcorn into a serving dish, and spoon over the prepared topping. Serve garnished with a lime wedge to squeeze over the seafood topping and sprinkle with strips of rind.

Sweet'n'Sour Snap Dragons

For a real laugh, hand round some chopsticks with this dish, guaranteed to get any party going with a swing.

★ 1 L/1³/₄ pts freshly popped popcorn

FOR THE TOPPING
★ 30 ml/2 tbsp sunflower or corn oil
★ 1 onion, peeled and chopped
★ 1 green pepper, deseeded and chopped

★ 1 carrot, peeled and cut into very thin julienne strips
★ 1 x 200 g/7 oz can pineapple
★ 5 g/1 tsp cornflour
★ 15 ml/1 tbsp soy sauce
★ 15 ml/1 tbsp white wine vinegar

Pop the popcorn in a large heavy-based pan as previously described, just before required.

Heat the oil in a pan then sauté the onion and green pepper for 5 minutes or until soft.

Meanwhile, blanch the carrot in boiling water, leave for 3 minutes then drain and add to the pan.

Drain and finely chop the pineapple, reserving the juice. Add to the pan.

Blend the cornflour with the reserved pineapple juice, the soy sauce and vinegar and stir into the pan. Bring to the boil.

Heat, stirring continuously until the mixture thickens then cook for a further 1 minute. Allow to cool slightly.

Place the freshly popped popcorn into a serving bowl then top with the prepared topping and serve.

77

POPCORN LOLLIES

**TRY PUTTING ONE OF THESE FUN LOLLIES
IN THE "TO GO" BAGS AT THE END OF A KIDS' PARTY.**

MAKES ABOUT **4-6** DEPENDING ON
THE SIZE OF THE MOULDS.
* 1 L/1^3/$_4$ pts freshly popped
  popcorn

* 225 g/8 oz plain toffees
* 30 ml/2 tbsp milk
* 2 tbsp/25 g/1 oz butter
* 5 g/1 tsp vanilla essence

Pop the popcorn in a large
heavy-based pan as previously
described, just before required.

Unwrap the toffees and place in
a heavy-based pan together with
the milk, butter and the vanilla
essence.

Heat gently, stirring occasionally
until the toffees have melted.

Remove from the heat, allow to
cool slightly and stir in the
freshly popped popcorn.

Leave until cool enough to
handle, then place in lightly-oiled
lolly moulds and place the sticks
in position. Leave until set
before removing.

78

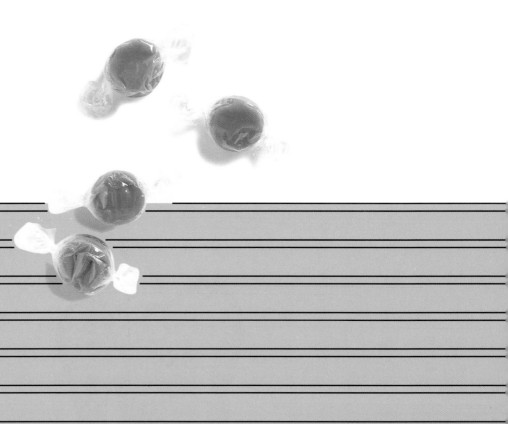

STRAWBERRY SUNDAE

TRY THIS FUN DESSERT IN THE SUMMER WHEN STRAWBERRIES ARE PLENTIFUL. IN THE WINTER, USE CHOPPED CANNED FRUIT OR SEEDLESS GRAPES.

★ 350 ml/12 fl oz freshly popped popcorn
★ 45 g/3 tbsp strawberry jam
★ 15 ml/1 tbsp lemon juice

★ 350 g/12 oz fresh strawberries, hulled and cut in half if large
★ scoops of vanilla ice cream

Pop the popcorn in a large heavy-based pan as previously described, just before required.

Heat the jam with the lemon juice and stir until smooth. Remove from the heat and allow to cool slightly.

Stir in the freshly popped popcorn and mix gently until well coated.

Layer the popcorn, strawberries and ice cream in tall sundae glasses and top with a final scoop of ice cream.

Decorate sundaes with a few pieces of popcorn and leftover strawberries.

79

INDEX